Contents

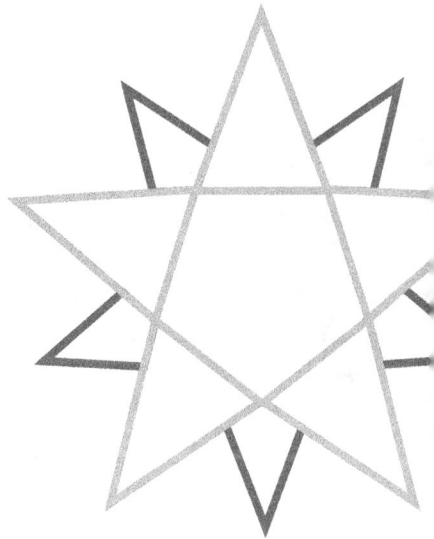

Foreword: Your Mission

You are about to start something that may change how you feel about yourself and your ability to lead.

You're going to learn how to let your best qualities radiate into the workplace and the world so people get who you are and what you have to offer.

This book exists because if you're like many people, you've been taught how to achieve, but not how to demonstrate your abilities in a way that creates the career you dream about.

Even fantastically gifted people need to learn to maximize their talents and steer the direction of their careers.

So, this book is about leading. It's about taking everything you know about yourself and deepening it so you can be someone who readily innovates, inspires and delivers.

This book will show you how to burst through your personal limitations and constantly grow. You will learn how to be the kind of person whose value is so wildly, vividly evident that you stand out from the crowd. You shine.

And when you shine you can write a ticket for any opportunity you desire. Any opportunity.

That's what it means to be a RockStar Leader.

Rock On,

Lisa

Lisa Martin, PCC

Part One:

WHY ROCKSTAR LEADERS ROCK

A RockStar Story

When Sam hired me in spring 2008 he was floundering, worried and visibly overwhelmed. Despite a history of success, he felt he wasn't living up to his potential. For the first time in his life he was insecure about his career.

I have an eye for talent and saw Sam's RockStar potential instantly. He had begun his career in corporate communications and later became a lobbyist. By the time I met him he was a vice president at a prestigious American university, responsible for public relations and advocacy in Washington.

Anyone looking at Sam's life could see he had an amazing career, but he only saw uncertainty.

If you remember back to mid-2008, we were starting to see indicators of a major shift in the economy. Sam worried this could spell disaster for his job. He feared a layoff and looming financial hardship.

The very first thing I advised him was to stop feeling victimized by the economy. I challenged him to start seeing himself as a victor. We worked together to identify some proactive steps he could take to be undeniably valuable at his workplace.

Fast-forward 6 months. Sam found himself smack dab in the midst of economic chaos and at the start of a long, enduring recession. But his career was booming. He'd just been recruited and promoted to chief of staff at a major American Museum Complex and Research Organization.

This is what happens when you focus on honing your skills as a RockStar Leader. Your talents shine no matter what's happening in the outside world. You create opportunities that match your biggest aspirations.

I call this value security. It's a new kind of career security built for uncertain times.

How RockStar Leaders Shine

Try as you might you can't control the ups and downs of the market. But if you choose to, you can turn up the volume on the value you deliver at work.

You can hone your performance, advance your leadership skills and take control of the results you deliver. All of this will, without question, make you shine more vividly.

And the brighter you shine, the more options you have in life. Think of it as star power.

Employers take notice of people who shine. They actively seek to retain and advance them, knowing the organization will benefit in spades.

RockStar Leaders are valued because:

> **They deliver.** Exceptional results are their norm.

> **They innovate.** Their ideas bring revenue, cost-efficiency and ease.

> **They inspire.** They exude positivity. People follow their lead.

The RockStar Economy

So here's the harsh reality: contrary to common belief, being a high achiever isn't enough to compete in this economy or position yourself for your ideal career.

Of course you need to be great at what you do. But you also have to make your talents visible.

Let's be clear, I'm not advocating shameless self-promotion or anything remotely like it.

I'm simply saying people who walk their dream career path are those who understand that **their performance is their currency.** If your performance isn't visible to those around you, you're bankrupt.

It wasn't always like this. Employers used to value tenure above all else. They retained and promoted people mostly based on seniority.

Clearly those days are gone. The whole idea of 'job security' now feels like a quaint memory of yesteryear.

The current economy rewards 'value security.' This is when your value in the workplace is unmistakably evident to those around you. Value security gives you unlimited options, regardless of market conditions.

It means that the people in your business world (your employer, your clients and beyond) really see who you are and quickly understand why it's essential to have you around.

RockStar Leaders aren't visible for the sake of attracting attention. They don't worry about saying witty things at meetings, hob-knobbing or inserting themselves into high-profile projects.

Being a RockStar Leader is about delivering clear value in the workplace and letting that be seen.

Part Two:

SET THE STAGE FOR ROCKSTAR LEADERSHIP

The Method

RockStar leadership skills can be learned by anyone, no matter where you are in your leadership journey.

The structure of this book is based on a self-coaching model to help you develop greater self-awareness and apply these skills in your everyday life.

In this book you will find:

1 **The RockStar Leader Model** that highlights the 6 skills required to be a RockStar Leader.

2 An explanation of each **RockStar Leader Skill** and why it matters.

3 **Four Advice Articles for each RockStar Leader Skill** to help you deepen your understanding.

4 **One Leading Question for each RockStar Leader Skill** to help you gain self-awareness.

5 **(Optional) RockStar Leader Assessment.**

The Model

Let me introduce you to the **RockStar Leader Model.**

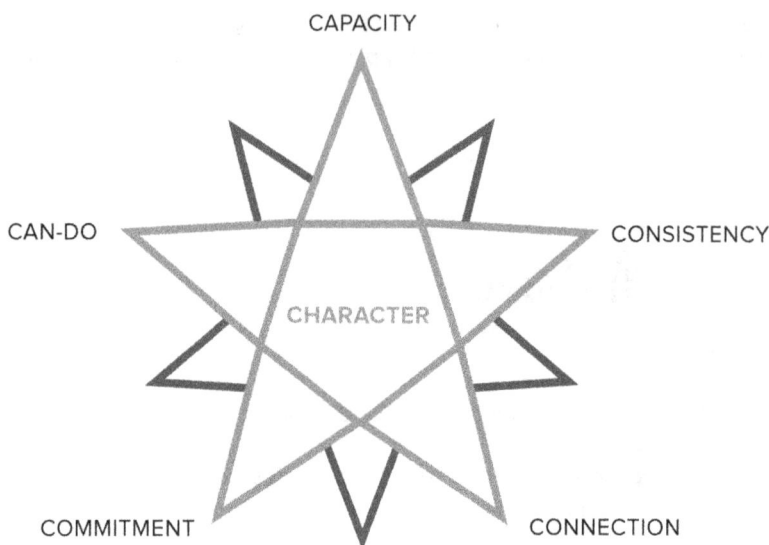

This model is based on 15 years of leadership coaching in a vast cross-section of industries across North America. In that time, I've delivered hundreds of workshops, coached thousands of people in senior roles and conducted in-depth interviews with countless leaders.

This model is also informed by my personal history as a corporate executive and the founder of three successful companies (see 'Acknowledgements' on page 92 for more detail).

Through all of this I've learned what distinguishes RockStar Leaders from the rest. It's abundantly clear to me that people who practice the following skills are those who rise through the ranks, land the careers they dream about, and create endless options for themselves. People with these skills are valued and rewarded most by employers.

Without further ado, here are the 6 Skills to Be a RockStar Leader:

1 **Capacity:** Manage major demands and stress.

2 **Consistency:** Deliver constant value by maximizing personal strengths.

3 **Connection:** Build real relationships and communicate with clarity.

4 **Commitment:** Find genuine passion for your work.

5 **Can-Do:** Be a force of positivity.

6 **Character:** Pursue success with integrity.

Make each RockStar Leader Skill your own, bringing it to life in a way that reflects the real you. The skills will only work for you if you steadily practice and improve all of them equally. They are an integrated system. Ignoring some in favor of others will limit your ability to shine.

Being a RockStar Leader means that you are committed to constantly growing. This doesn't mean you have to climb the corporate ladder to its highest rung. That's up to you. It simply means you're progressively making bigger contributions to the organization for which you work.

Part Three:

THE 6 ROCKSTAR LEADER SKILLS

Capacity

Capacity is your ability to cope with and manage all aspects of your life.

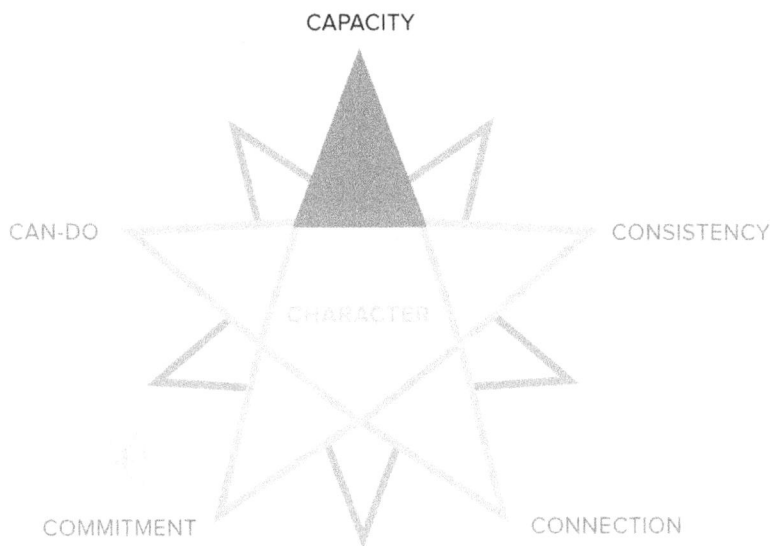

CAPACITY

CAN-DO

CONSISTENCY

CHARACTER

COMMITMENT

CONNECTION

For example, if you're living at **optimal capacity**, you're easily managing your workload, physical fitness, personal relationships, emotions and spiritual health. If something unexpected gets thrown at you, you adapt quickly without enduring lots of stress.

Most people are not functioning at optimal capacity. It's both an art and a science. As you read about this skill, be brutally honest with yourself so you can gain the insight to shift to your own optimal capacity.

Most people are either 'under capacity' or 'above capacity.'

If you're **under capacity**, you spend a lot of time on things that aren't a high priority to you and that aren't leading you to the life you want. You often wonder where all the hours in the day have gone. At the end of the day, you feel frustrated that few important items on your to-do list are completed. It's not that you're not busy, because you might be. But there are gaps in your productivity.

If you're **above capacity**, you likely feel like your life is always in fifth gear. The term 'wired' might apply to you. You often feel like you're doing many things at the same time. Moments of quiet reflection are rare. You are always 'on.' Sure, you're productive but you're on the verge of burning out. You're operating at a pace that's not healthy or sustainable.

So let's break down the 7 Elements of Capacity:

1 **Worthiness:** Loving who you are.

2 **Emotional & Spiritual Well-Being:** Seeing the bigger picture, handling whatever comes your way.

3 **Physical Self-Care:** Taking care of your body.

4 **Relational Vitality:** Being deeply connected to the people you love, feeling part of a community.

5 **Personal Growth:** Feeling energized about your life and where you're going.

6 **Environmental Management:** Having a sense of control of your surroundings.

7 **Self-Mastery:** A balanced, flowing life. Easily managing new things that come along.

About the 7 Elements of Capacity

The pyramid below illustrates how the **7 Elements of Capacity** build on each other, creating your capacity to **shine.**

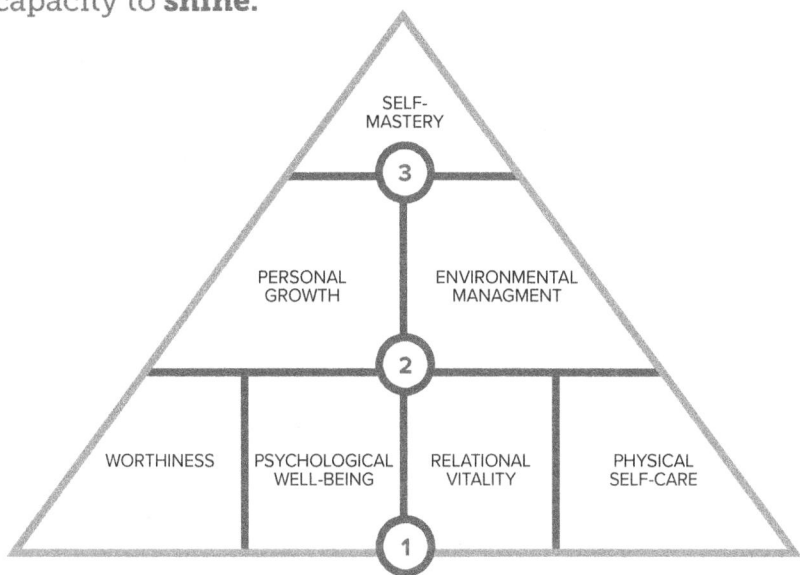

```
                    SELF-
                   MASTERY
                     (3)

      PERSONAL          ENVIRONMENTAL
       GROWTH             MANAGMENT
                     (2)

WORTHINESS   PSYCHOLOGICAL   RELATIONAL   PHYSICAL
             WELL-BEING       VITALITY    SELF-CARE
                     (1)
```

LEVEL 1 Basics: Without these basic elements of personal wellness in place, it's not possible to be at optimal capacity. You're running on empty if you don't have these covered.

LEVEL 2 Build: With the basics of personal wellness in place, you're now in a position to be in charge of your circumstances and to focus on personal growth.

LEVEL 3 Bonus: Once you're in charge of your circumstances and you've got a clear road map for personal growth, you're ready to have a balanced, flowing life. You're able to take on whatever life hands you.

Leadership: How Much Can You Handle?

As a leader you're either 'under capacity,' 'above capacity' or at 'optimal capacity.'

Sometimes when I first describe this concept to people, I see a glint in their eyes when I mention 'above capacity.' Perfectionists, I'm looking right at you. So, I'd like to frame this to help you see the dangers of not operating in your optimal zone.

> **Under Capacity:** Not reaching your potential

> **Optimal Capacity:** Maximizing your potential

> **Above Capacity:** Compromising your potential

So, are you functioning at your optimal capacity?

If you are, you're easily managing work, fitness and relationships with family and friends. You're managing your emotions and spiritual well-being. If something unexpected gets tossed at you, you adapt quickly without experiencing great stress.

Being at optimal capacity is much more than meeting deadlines and getting glowing performance reviews. It's about replenishing your body, mind and spirit so you can continually perform. It's about balancing action and rest.

Every RockStar Leader needs to have a keen eye on their personal 'replenishment plan,' or they may be headed to burnout. And trust me, I know whereof I speak.

To assess if you're at optimal capacity, read the following statements and note how many are true for you:

1 I spend time with the people who are important to me and whose company I enjoy.

2 I give myself the same love and attention I give to others.

3 I exercise regularly and eat healthy meals.

4 I feel rejuvenated when I wake up in the morning.

5 I can bounce back from almost anything.

6 When a curve ball comes my way, I respond calmly and without anger.

7 Outside of my work, my life has meaning.

If 6 or 7 of these statements feel very true for you, well done. You're operating at (or very close to) optimal capacity and your intention should be to find ways to stay in this zone.

If 5 or less of these statements feel very true for you, it's time to examine how you are balancing action with replenishment. You are either 'above' or 'under' your ideal capacity.

Start a Rejuvenation Program

As a leader you need time and space for rejuvenation and personal growth. This is common sense. So, why do so many leaders neglect to take the time?

Lack of capacity is the biggest reason. It stems from a belief that the world as you know it will end if you take time for rest and reflection. Projects will come to a screeching halt, your staff will wander aimless and confused through your office corridors, customers will freak out en masse.

It's helpful to let go of the idea that giving yourself time to rejuvenate is somehow a disservice to society. This is a myth that has led many people to the dark, dismal corner of the corporate universe known as burnout. Do not follow in their footsteps.

You're human. You need breathing room to pursue new thinking, process information and make needed changes in yourself. If it takes every ounce of your energy to just get through the day, you'll never find breathing room. You'll never evolve.

The biggest piece of advice I can offer is simply to schedule in rejuvenation time. I mean that literally. Pull up your calendar and schedule in time for workouts, walks in nature, journaling, spa days, weekend getaways, meditation, hiking...whatever restores you.

I have a client who scheduled monthly massages on her calendar and another who allotted weekly playground time with his son. Inevitably I see the same results again and again. When people make downtime a true priority, their stress level visibly drops. Their sense of ease comes back, along with their sense of humor. Next thing you know, they're making decisions more swiftly. Tensions ease at home and work.

Treat your rejuvenation program with the same importance you give other commitments. If you don't take it seriously and you constantly postpone these vital activities, your capacity for work and life will start to wane.

If your rejuvenation program is really humming, you'll find yourself with an expanding capacity for all aspects of your life. You'll be a more clear-headed, productive, energized leader.

Perfectionism is Not Your Friend: **Doing Less Really is More**

News alert: perfectionism is not your friend.

Perfectionism will tell you need to do more, more and more. It will tell you that you're not good enough, but maybe you will be if you just push yourself a little bit harder.

The reality is, doing more doesn't always lead to achieving more or having more. Anyone who's ever been burnt out will tell you this. You can be incredibly busy, running in a million directions all at the same time, and at the end of the day look back and say, 'I'm exhausted and I have no idea what my purpose is.'

Sometimes you gotta slow down before you can speed up.

And sometimes you simply need to take on less stuff. I'm continually meeting high-achieving people who seem to believe they have limitless capacity.

I get it. I used to believe that too. You keep adding more and more stuff into your work life and home life, but you can't figure out why you're still unsatisfied.

I'll tell you why: you are exceeding your capacity. As talented and powerful as you are, you're still human. You need downtime. You need room to breathe. And yes, sometimes you need fewer things to do in a day. There's no shame in that.

Where did anyone ever get the idea that as you move through adulthood you can just keep piling on more and more responsibilities...and somehow you'll continually expand your capacity to handle it all?

It's a lie.

I'm not saying 'you can't have it all.' I'm saying you can't have it all at the same time. Life is a highway, people. Let it unfold gradually rather than trying to pile everything at once.

Perhaps the most classic example of this is the high-achiever who becomes a parent for the first time. Now operating on little to no sleep with the joy, stress and chaos that comes with having a newborn, our achiever now wants to land a promotion at work and berates herself/himself for not working out as frequently.

When major life change happens, be compassionate with yourself. As you take on more in one part of your life, let up on yourself in another part for a while. This doesn't mean you disregard your career and your personal health if you have a child, for example. It just means you may need to adjust your expectations of yourself.

The myth of perfectionism is that you're giving all of yourself to everything you do. The reality is you're spinning your wheels doing too many things and no aspect of your life is experienced fully.

The thing I want you to consider is: sometimes less really is more.

That Nagging Feeling: *'I want to do more with my life'*

Is there a chance that you're living beneath your true capacity?

If so, there's no disgrace in that. I see talented, driven people all the time who aren't living up to their capacity.

It doesn't mean you're lazy or unambitious. It doesn't mean you're not successful at what you do. So, let's take those notions right off the table.

Being under capacity means that you'd like to be doing more with your life, personally and/or professionally, but something is getting in your way. Most likely, *you're* getting in your way and you don't even know it.

Often when people feel a sense of aimlessness about their lives, or a sense of exasperation at not knowing what their true purpose is, these are clues that they have untapped capacity.

In my experience, this issue tends to go undiagnosed. I've seen people live this way for decades before understanding the problem. It can be debilitating.

I want you to know discovering you're functioning under capacity is a fabulous thing, if you allow it to be. It means that your life is about to open up. It means that, if you're brave enough to go on a journey of self-discovery and embrace change, anything is possible.

I truly mean this. I see it happen all the time.

So, be real with yourself. Here are 7 statements to consider. How many of these feel true for you?

1 I see opportunities all around me but I don't often act on them.

2 I spend time with whoever wants to spend time with me.

3 I would like to feel a deeper sense of community.

4 I feel stuck.

5 I'd like to develop new attitudes and behaviors.

6 I'd like to be different in the future.

7 A lot of my time is unfocused.

If 4 or more of these statements feel true for you, you may be living beneath your capacity. It could be high time to start a journey to discover what will make you fully shine.

If 3 or fewer of these statements feel true, your next step is to explore if you are at 'optimal capacity' (i.e., maximizing your potential) or 'exceeding your capacity' (i.e., compromising your potential).

Capacity

LEADING QUESTION

What activities most rejuvenate me?

Consistency

Consistency is knowing your leadership brand and delivering on it.

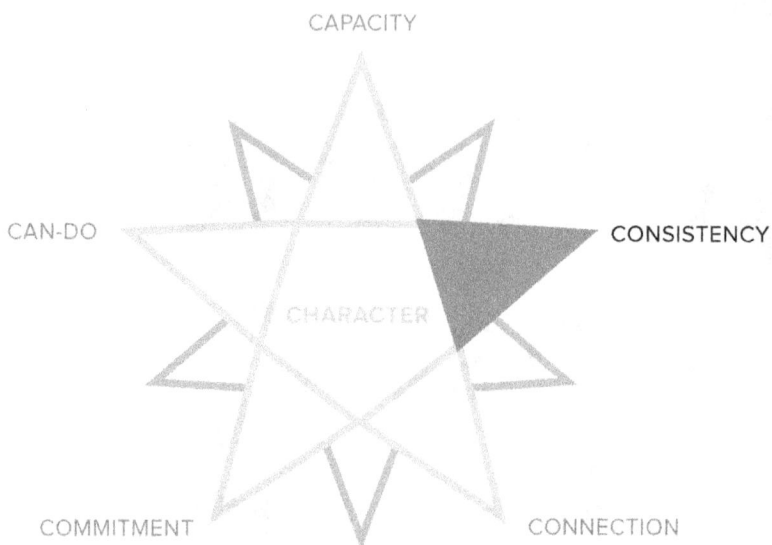

CAPACITY

CAN-DO

CONSISTENCY

CHARACTER

COMMITMENT

CONNECTION

It's the promise of what you will consistently contribute to your organization. It's about understanding your brilliance, your extraordinary qualities and the results you will achieve.

Simply put, it's a promise kept.

But sometimes it's hard to know what you're brilliant at. These abilities come so naturally to you that you may not even recognize them as strengths and talents.

I've seen people with incredible aptitude for numbers shake their heads in frustration when others can't keep up with their calculations. Math is so second nature to them, they can't even imagine someone else's mind could operate without that same proficiency.

These abilities are your **superpowers.** They are the wondrous feats your mind performs with ease while others must use brute force.

Your leadership brand also includes the special aspects of your personality that make you ... you. These are your **superqualities.**

For example, you may be an outrageously talented project manager whose superpowers are tracking fine details and foreseeing obstacles. But maybe you're also naturally comedic with the gift of the gab – and these qualities mean that your team adores you and they're motivated to go the extra mile.

Last but not least, to have a solid leadership brand you need to clearly define what results people can expect from you. Your **major results** must align directly with what your organization and the people in it truly need.

Having a leadership brand allows you to focus your efforts appropriately and it keeps you accountable to yourself and others.

YOUR SUPERPOWERS

The 3 brilliant abilities that come second nature to you.

+

YOUR SUPERQUALITIES

Your 3 extraordinary personal qualities.

+

YOUR MAJOR RESULTS

The value you deliver.

=

LEADERSHIP BRAND

You'll know you're on the right track with the articulation of your leadership brand when it syncs up with how others see you.

Are You Annoyed? Congrats, You Just Discovered Your Superpower

There's a really amusing trick I've discovered. Whenever one of my clients is profoundly agitated (read: steam emitting from ears) because someone on their team NEVER does a certain task in the 'right' way, I know I have struck gold. This task is my client's superpower.

A superpower is something you do with such ease and ability it's like breathing. It's so second nature that it doesn't even occur to you that it's a talent, or that other people can't do it just as easily.

HUGE HINT: If you are always annoyed at the way someone else does a certain thing and you want to snatch it away from them so you can do it 'right,' hello – that's probably your superpower.

Knowing your superpowers makes life in the work world so much smoother. It lets you focus on the things that come most naturally to you, and it makes you far more compassionate when others try to do them.

If, for example, you are a marketing director who is a wizard at editing, I promise you, you will be unable to stop yourself from re-editing content that was already edited by someone else.

will be far more efficient and harmonious for everyone if you simply assign yourself the task of editing and re-organize your team accordingly.

If you're a sales manager who is genius at closing deals ... FOCUS ON CLOSING. Please. Save yourself and everyone else the aggravation of trying to do it as well as you.

If you can't do all the closing, you need to scale your team with others who have this superpower. Let those who are great at getting the first meeting and building relationships focus on these tasks ... these are different but equally awesome superpowers.

Most people have roughtly 3 true superpowers. So pay close attention to your irritation level. It could be a potent insight into who you are and what makes you remarkable.

Here are 3 things to watch for:

1 What task(s) do you continually find yourself coaching people to do 'correctly?'

2 What task(s) do you redo or refine even when the most talented person on your team has attempted it?

3 What task(s) are you incredulous that it takes others so long to do?

Be Distinct:
Personality Matters

I want to discuss the subject of 'superqualities.'

Superqualities are the aspects of your personality that really make you, you. Sure, your organization may employ several accountants, project managers or sales reps that all have a role quite similar to yours.

But the way you do your job – the unique qualities you bring to it – will be distinct from everyone else.

Knowing your superqualities is a vital way to distinguish yourself in the workplace and in the world. It allows you to consciously put these natural traits to use. Just as importantly, it allows you to stop trying to be someone you're not.

People sometimes assume that extroverted, charismatic personalities are always the most valued. In my experience as a corporate executive, I can tell you it isn't true.

In reality, it takes an assortment of people each with distinct qualities to make a kick-ass team. If everyone is the life of the party, nothing gets done.

So, instead of trying to bring out qualities in yourself you perceive to be leadership-worthy, notice and leverage the qualities that people already value in you.

One of my clients was convinced he possessed no 'superqualities.' Tried though he might, he thought nothing about his personality really stood out.

I asked him to pay attention to situations in his life where he felt a sense of ease and situations when people really engaged with him. I asked him to notice what traits he was exhibiting in those cases.

So he started paying attention. He was struck by how comfortable he felt when people treated him as a confidant, and how frequently this happened. He noted his ability to communicate easily in these situations, providing a patient ear and sage counsel. He realized it was natural for him to see things from other people's perspectives. To be empathetic. To be grounded.

t didn't take long for him to realize compassion, trust-worthiness and a calm demeanor were his superqualities.

Be super-cautious not to mistake common positive attributes with your superqualities.

For example, all of the project managers at your company may be highly organized. That's a great attribute, but it's one that is expected of a project manager...just as anyone would expect an accountant to be thorough or an HR manager to be relatable.

Here are 3 exercises to help you brainstorm your superqualities:

1 Write a list of 5 - 6 words that best describe your personality. Use words that really get to the heart of who you are.

2 What have other people said are your best qualities? Think back...consider what family members, friends and colleagues have said.

3 What 5 - 6 characteristics do you value most in yourself? Maybe you're someone who is always punctual or who has superb listening skills. Maybe you value your honesty, sense of compassion or diligence.

After you do this brainstorming, narrow down your list to the 3 superqualities that most define you.

The Brass Tacks:
Leadership Equals Results

I've heard people equate leadership with strategic thinking, or motivational skills or a visionary mind. All of these things are fabulous, but none of them is the defining element of leadership.

Leadership, very simply, is about results. Can you get the results you say you're going to get? Can you get the results people expect from you?

If not, nothing else really matters.

Now, I'm not saying get results at any cost. I'm not Machiavelli. Without question, you want to be a leader with integrity and values. I'm just saying if there are no results, it's all for naught.

When I coach people on improving their leadership skills, I always talk about 'knowing your results.' I see so many talented people exhausting themselves with too many ill-defined projects and commitments. The end of a quarter comes along and although they've worked their butts off, they're hard pressed to explain what they've accomplished.

To be a RockStar Leader, you need to get uber-smart about what you're taking on and then go above and beyond what's expected. Soon you will be known for what you've achieved every quarter, every year. That's how you build a RockStar leadership brand.

Here are 4 questions to help you start to zero in on your results:

1 Who do you serve in your organization? (i.e., who are your internal and external customers)?

2 What major results have you delivered in the past 12 months?

3 What results would allow you to generate the maximum value for the people you serve? (i.e., what do they really, really want from you?)

4 What major results can you deliver in the next 12 months?

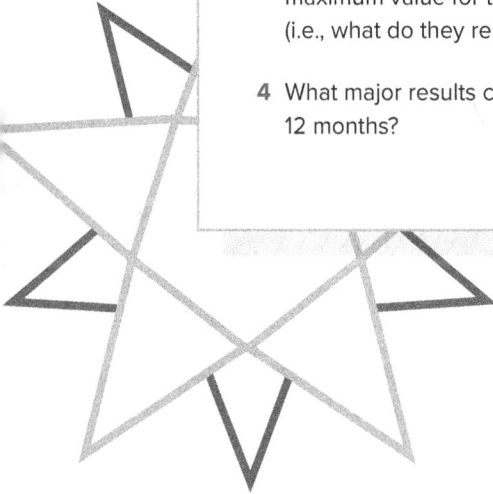

Define Yourself as a Leader

There is no single, definitive way to be a RockStar Leader. You can certainly learn by example but trying to adopt someone else's leadership style will never work in the long run.

I'm a huge believer in defining your own leadership brand. I get how odd and disconcerting it may feel to see yourself as a 'brand,' but go with me because – applied correctly – the concept is really powerful.

If I ask most people to name what they are most brilliant at (their superpowers), they are likely to hesitate or tell me about the skills they think are most exciting or marketable.

If I were to ask you what personality traits really make you... you, you might find it hard to narrow it down to just 2 or 3 that really set you apart.

I find that many people think of their brand as the role they play in an organization – as in, I'm the VP of marketing or the director of sales.

But a leadership brand is not a title. It's a promise. It's a promise of how you will use your unique abilities and traits to deliver results that people can count on.

Knowing who you are is fundamental to becoming a RockStar Leader. It helps you zero in on exactly how to invest your energy to make the biggest impact rather than taking a scattershot approach.

It also makes it abundantly clear how to differentiate yourself within your organization. There may be many people who play a similar role, but none will have the same leadership brand as you.

Sample Leadership Brands

Example 1:

"I am known as [*superqualities:* **a compassionate, clear-headed, fun-loving**] HR director who [*major results:* **recruits top talent**] and has an exceptional ability to [*superpowers:* **resolve interpersonal problems, see hidden potential and facilitate meetings.**]"

Example 2:

"I am known as a [*superqualities:* **visionary, straight-shooting, organized**] sales manager who [*major results:* **exceeds quarterly goals**] and has an exceptional ability to [*superpowers:* **break the ice, connect people and get contracts signed.**]"

Consistency

LEADING QUESTION

What personal traits and talents make me a compelling leader?

Connection

Connection is your ability to create caring, meaningful and mutually rewarding relationships. It's about having people around you that support your dreams, just as you support theirs. This is vital to success in business and life.

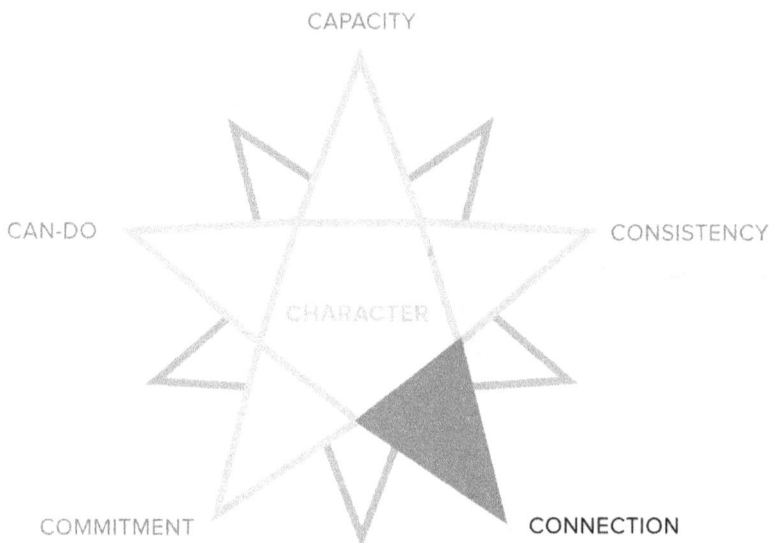

CAPACITY

CAN-DO

CONSISTENCY

CHARACTER

COMMITMENT

CONNECTION

Being a great connector isn't about knowing everyone in town or being a social butterfly. It's not about wowing people with your personal network, charisma or talent. Great connectors are people who genuinely care about other people. They inspire people to believe in themselves and their ability to contribute to the world.

If you want to make strong **connections** you need to focus on other people and their needs. You have to look beyond your own goals and listen carefully for others' aspirations. People take action for their own reasons, so learn to see things from other people's point of view. Not only will you grow from the knowledge of others, you'll get more done. People will be far more likely to rally behind your projects and causes if they know you are truly in their court.

To be a great connector you need to:

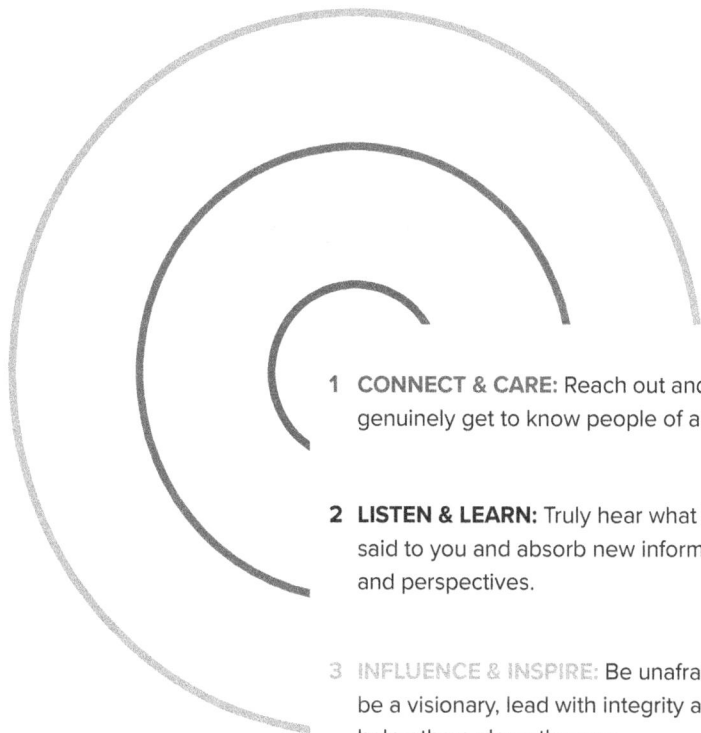

1 **CONNECT & CARE:** Reach out and genuinely get to know people of all types.

2 **LISTEN & LEARN:** Truly hear what is being said to you and absorb new information and perspectives.

3 INFLUENCE & INSPIRE: Be unafraid to be a visionary, lead with integrity and help others along the way.

RockStar leadership isn't about drawing attention to yourself and your amazing skills. It's about helping others have faith in themselves and their own abilities. As a leader, your job is to help individuals and organizations get exactly where they want to go, finding your own success along the way.

Are You Truly Listening?

Most people believe they are listening when others talk. But of course believing something doesn't make it real.

We live in a society where it's common to read an incoming text or email while sitting across the table from someone.

You may find yourself scanning the news while you're on a conference call, or mentally preparing for one meeting while sitting in another.

You might even praise yourself for your multi-tasking talents and supreme levels of efficiency. But your 'efficiency' comes at a cost.

Your to-do list might be shorter but you're sacrificing real moments of human connection. Is this the choice you want to make?

People with strong relationships get farther in life and work, and they're happier for it.

Success doesn't come from a completed to-do list. It comes from fully experiencing your life and the people in it. This can't be done without heartfelt connection.

If you are really listening when people speak, you hear far more than just words. You tune into subtext, which is often far more important. You hear unspoken concerns and challenges. You're aware of the hidden interests and talents of people around you.

And you just know people better. It's one thing to have pleasant, polite relationships. It's another to see the unique light that shines in each person and to feel a true connection.

So, back to my original question ... are you really listening?

Here are a few statements to help you see if you are listening. How true is each statement for you?

1 In conversation, I focus on others and their needs, not just my own.

2 I quiet my thoughts when others are speaking.

3 I resist the urge to plan my response when others are speaking.

4 I make sure I've understood what someone has said by confirming it with them.
(i.e. 'So what I'm hearing you say is ... ').

5 I consciously listen beneath the surface of what is being said so I can understand unstated concerns.

No matter how strong your current listening skills are, I urge you to take them further. This is a crucial skill to shining as a leader.

3 Ways to Advance Your Listening

Sound expert and TED talker, Julian Treasure, believes we are losing our listening.

He says the visual and auditory cacophony that bombards us daily is wearing us thin. We're too tired to listen.

Our poor brains are overwhelmed with digital stimulation. Quieting our minds to simply listen intently to another human being is becoming harder and harder.

Treasure says that without keen listening, we lose the ability to understand each other. And where is this world headed with less understanding?

Here are 3 tips for listening better:

1 Reality Check

It's far too easy to gloss over the substance of what someone is saying because you think you've gotten the basic gist. The gist often isn't enough. Probe for a clearer understanding with phrases like:

> Say more about that.

> What do you mean when you say X?

> You've mentioned X twice. Tell me what is important about that?

2 Feel Your Way

Words are only one aspect of communication. Notice the emotion underlying the words. For example:

> Is the speaker's lack of excitement conveying doubt about the success of a project?

> Is their annoyance telling you they are angry at your behavior or someone else's?

> Is their exuberance a sign that they're the right person to lead the charge on a certain task?

3 Go Deep

People don't always tell you their 'whole story' head on. They may be only giving you surface information (think tip of the iceberg) when their values and true beliefs may be hidden from your view. They may be hinting at something important, hoping you will read their cues. You may need to tune in closely to unlock the real information they want to convey. Seek their unstated concerns and clarify the context in which they view the situation or your comments. Reflect back what you hear them say. Then people will feel truly heard. Here are examples of how that can look:

> We've discussed the next steps we need to take to complete the project. What do you feel is the best way to proceed?

> What do you feel the risks are? What do you feel are the benefits?

> What makes you say that?

Is Ambition in Your Way?

Here's something to consider: is ambition preventing you from being a great leader?

I believe leadership is about people first, goals second...because you won't achieve any goals without people on your side.

Ambition has a nasty way of tainting relationships. If it's unchecked, it's a sure-fire way to limit your abilities as a leader.

I often encounter people who are preoccupied with being popular at work. Others spend inordinate amounts of time trying to get in good with the higher ups.

People that really get the importance of relationship-building know it's not about currying favor or leveraging influence. Quite the opposite.

A few years ago I worked with a client who was very nearly obsessed with being seen with the 'right' people at work and careful to position herself as a mover and shaker.

What she was unconscious of, however, was how unkindly she treated colleagues she deemed 'not strategic' to her ambitions. The reality was, she'd earned a reputation as a snob. Miffed colleagues were slow to make her projects a priority, and she couldn't see why.

As we worked together she began to notice how she treated people, and I'll tell you, she was mortified. She wasn't compassionless. And she wasn't a snob. She was simply blinded (and foiled) by her own ambition.

She altered her behaviour quickly, but it took time to garner trust. Eventually as people saw her sincerity, it became easier and faster for her to rally support and get projects done.

The moral here, is that to connect with people you have to get out of your own head and think beyond your own aspirations. You need to start truly understanding those around you and what motivates them on an individual level.

You know you've got great relationships when people are inspired to take action because they feel personally committed to your ideas.

You're a true connector when people know you believe in them. They know you want what's in their best interest, not just your own.

When people see you this way, trust arises. And from that trust, there's a willingness to help.

Ask yourself these questions to assess if ambition is in your way:

1 Do you mostly connect with people for a strategic purpose rather than out of genuine interest?

2 After you meet someone new do you think about how that person might be useful to you in the future?

3 Do you tend to disregard people if you think they're not in a position to help you?

If you answered 'yes' to any of these questions, it's time to start examining the priority you place on ambition. Reconsider the importance of genuine human connection.

Build Genuine Relationships

If you want to be a great connector, you need to notice the people around you, ask questions, be open-hearted and, above all, listen.

Here are 5 questions to ask yourself:

1 Do you actively connect with many different types of people in your personal life?

2 Do you actively connect with people at all levels of your organization?

3 In work conversations, do you truly focus on relating to the other person or could your conversations be defined as transactional exchanges of information?

4 Are you open and honest with your colleagues?

5 Do you feel like people at work know the real you?

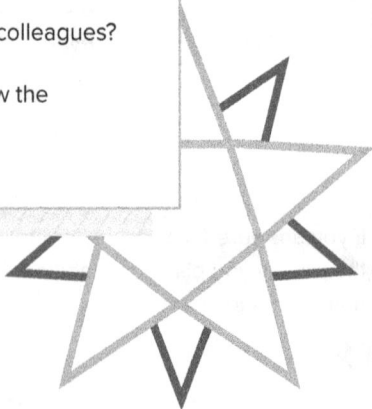

If you found yourself answering 'no' to some or all of these questions, working on your connection skills will take your leadership abilities to the next level. More than that, it will help you have more significant relationships with the people around you.

"If you cannot hear the sound of the genuine in you, you will all of your life spend your days on the ends of strings that somebody else pulls."

Howard Thurman

Connection

LEADING QUESTION

Do I genuinely care about the people I work with?

Commitment

Commitment to your job isn't something you can happily fake for long.

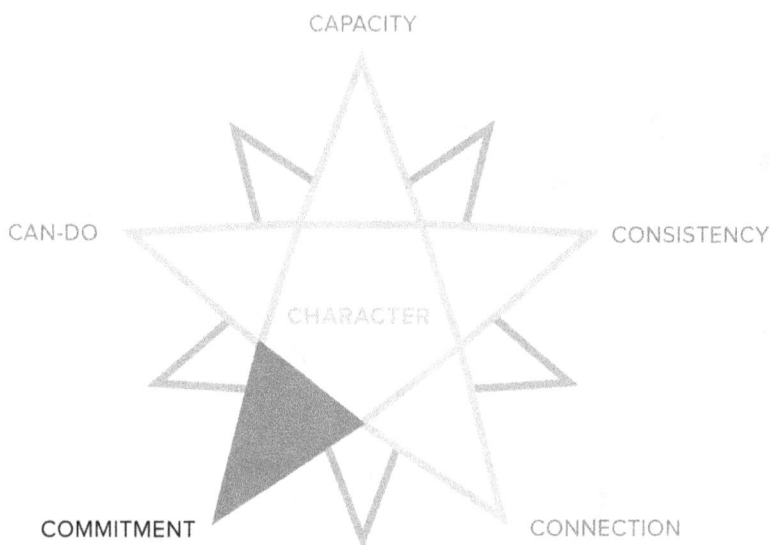

True, sustainable, fulfilling **commitment** comes from discovering how your personal purpose aligns to the mandate of your job and your organization. It is the greater reason you do your job: the bigger 'why.'

In other words, if your marketing job is just about leads, or your accounting job is just about numbers, your commitment will wane ... likely sooner than later.

If on the other hand, you have tuned into a greater purpose for your chosen career path and you know how your current job aligns to it, you won't even have to try to be committed. It will happen authentically.

For example, if you know that your purpose in life is to help people feel beautiful about themselves, your marketing job in the fashion industry takes on new life. If you know your purpose is to help people turn their wild ideas into thriving businesses, your **commitment** to accounting is transformed.

Commitment matters because people around you sense it. Even if you're tremendously talented and crazy productive, a lack of authentic commitment is palpable. There's a degree of trust that can only be attained when people sense your heart is really in it.

But this isn't just about other people and how they view you. This is about you living a life that you love and feeling connected to a purpose that actually matters to you.

Having a sense of **commitment** is foundational to feeling grounded and passionate about what you do. You can achieve a lot even if you don't have **commitment**, but your accomplishments won't ever feel as meaningful.

There are 5 measures of commitment:

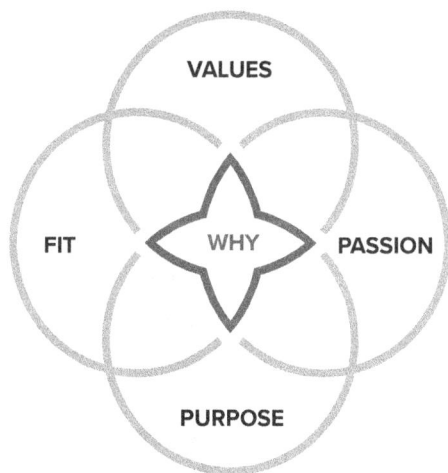

To have **commitment**, you need to know the greater reason you do what you do (the 'why'). That 'why' needs to inspire a genuine sense of passion in you and it needs to connect to your personal values and purpose. Being a RockStar Leader means you live your 'why' AND you are able to clearly see how your greater reason is aligned to your organization, your specific role and the outcomes you deliver.

Your Purpose on the Planet

Right now, I'd like you to ask yourself 3 revealing questions:

1 Do you sometimes feel discomfort with your life and you can't trace the cause?

2 Do you sometimes question what you're here on this planet to do?

3 Do you feel you're quietly waiting for something to happen to make the pieces of your life fit together and make sense?

If you answered 'yes' to any or all of these questions, the fix may be closer than you think. Sure, these can be symptoms of an existential crisis, but they can also be symptoms of something more earthly ... a life out of sync with your purpose.

Let's begin here. We're living in a society that would have us believe everyone is made deliriously happy by achieving exactly the same things: money, white picket fence, luxury car, good job, 2.5 kids, 2 week vacations in Maui and eternal beauty.

There's nothing wrong with any of these things. But if you're focusing your life (consciously or not) on having them, it's worth pausing to ask yourself — are these things bringing you the wholeness you expected to feel?

f not, let's continue. That feeling of wholeness I'm referring to is what you feel when your life is aligned to a greater purpose. It's when you know why you spend your life doing what you do.

When you know your 'why' and allow it to guide every personal and career decision you make, let me tell you, magic happens. It's a game-changer.

You feel strong and purposeful. You're connected to your life's unique meaning. You no longer struggle with who you are and what you're meant to do.

That icky, uncomfortable sense that something is wrong with your life but you don't know what it is just goes away.

Aligning your life with your 'why' doesn't mean you have to give up your material possessions or fabulous lifestyle. It just means that you're guided by something bigger.

What Would Steve Jobs Do?

Whenever I see someone struggling to find meaning and passion, I know they are seeking to uncover the bigger reason for their existence, even though they often don't realize it.

You can't feel purposeful, directed and fully you without knowing your bigger reason. Some people are lucky enough to just inherently know it early in life. Others need a bit of guidance to get there, and that's where I come in.

Steve Jobs' strengths and flaws have been analyzed ad nauseam, so I won't get into them here. But what I'm continually fascinated by is his ability – for better or worse – to live and lead according to his grand purpose. He had an unrelenting talent for this for which I personally strive.

There's a grainy, undated YouTube video of Jobs discussing the idea that 'people with passion can change the world for the better.' Even though he describes this as Apple's core value, it's clear it's more than that. It's his personal mission. Apple is simply how he manifested this in his business life.

Here's what I believe: If Jobs had not aligned his work to this personal mission, Apple as we know it would not exist today.

If, like many well-meaning CEOs do, he had chosen common corporate values like 'innovation' or 'exceptional customer service' or 'integrity,' I wouldn't be writing this story on my MacBook Pro or proof-reading it later on my iPad.

Jobs dug deep. He didn't let mistakes and failures water down his view. Even when he was booted from his own company and his career seemingly skidded way off course, he came back with an even clearer focus on his personal mission.

This is why — for individuals and for companies — deciding your bigger purpose in life is not an exercise to be taken lightly.

If you've been guilty of creating a personal mission statement and then shoving it in a binder somewhere never to be seen again, think of Steve Jobs. And go dig your mission out of that drawer. Or better yet, go through the exercise of creating it again with this new perspective in mind.

"It **(what you choose to do)** has got to be something that you're passionate about because otherwise you won't have the perseverance to see it through."

Steve Jobs

How to Find Your Core Values

The *Financial Times* defines values-based leadership as connecting your organization's goals to your personal values.

But personally, I love how **Forbes** describes it simply as 'doing the right thing,' in an article by Kellogg Professor Harry M. Jansen Kraemer Jr.

Here's a quote from that article:

"As I tell my students, becoming the best kind of leader isn't about emulating a role model or a historic figure. Rather, your leadership must be rooted in who you are and what matters most to you. When you truly know yourself and what you stand for, it is much easier to know what to do in any situation. It always comes down to doing the right thing and doing the best you can."

In this context, leadership is about diving deeply into your psyche and knowing yourself on a profound level. This is what being a RockStar Leader is all about.

Here's a framework to discover and live by your core values:

1 **First, don't confuse your core values with the values of your company.** This is about you. Your core values are what you value most above everything else. Not just at work, but in life.

   Get your head out of business matters. Sit in the park on the grass with your iPad or journal, and let your mind roam free.

   Play with words like passion, discovery, adventure, contribution, creativity and freedom (to name just a few).

   DO NOT ANALYZE. Analyzing will send you down the wrong path. Let this exercise be quick and painless. Just notice which words make your heart sing. Choose 4 that make it sing the loudest. Done!

2 **Make your 4 core values central to your life.** Start with simple things like posting them on your fridge or making them the background image on your computer. You need to see them constantly.

   As the stuff of life arises, requiring personal and business decisions, use your values as a filter. Ask yourself what decision will be most aligned with them. Trust yourself and your values. They will steer you in a direction of integrity and truth.

3 **Be authentic.** For example, if you choose 'adventure' as a core value, but you live a very conventional life and make only prudent, conservative business decisions ... you aren't living and leading by that core value. I'm not saying you need to be crazy and reckless. I'm just saying you need to live from a place that's authentic to who you are.

When you know your values, you'll make decisions and create plans that excite you. You'll lead others in a way that's more genuine. Your peers and your team will respond to you differently. It's far more empowering to lead from a place of clarity and strength rather than some standard ideal of what a leader should be.

Gut Check: **Are You Living Your Why?**

Knowing your 'why' is a huge trend in the business world, and I for one am a huge proponent of this (as you already know).

I never tire of seeing people become reinvigorated by their lives when I help them tune into and articulate their purpose, passion, values and how this aligns to everyday leading and living. It's like an inner light bulb turns on, illuminating their true essence.

But knowing your 'why' and living up to it are 2 different things.

Living it requires breaking old habits and being comfortable with making decisions that might unsettle other people.

If you're an established accountant who's just realized, for example, that creativity is part of your greater purpose, you might alarm people if you start pursuing your secret passion for painting.

To onlookers, that kind of realignment might seem rash. But it's not. You gotta be you to shine.

Having said this, living your 'why' doesn't necessarily require dramatic upheaval. It's mostly about the more subtle aspects of how you live and lead. It's about fit.

Let me help you get a quick gut check on how well you're currently living your 'why.'

Ask yourself the following questions...and please, be brutally honest:

1 Do I exude my 'why' in the way I speak?

2 Do I exude my 'why' in the way I present myself to the world?

3 Do I exude my 'why' in my career choices?

4 Do I exude my 'why' in the way I spend my free time?

5 Is my 'why' evident in my leadership style?

If you found you answered 'yes' more often than 'no,' kudos; you are shining brightly. If not, consider making some adjustments slowly, day by day, until you feel you are living your life in alignment with your 'why.' And you will feel empowered and full of life.

Commitment

LEADING QUESTION

How do I describe my 'why'?

Can-Do

If you're a **can-do** person, you have an inherent belief you can accomplish things in life. You have an unwavering sense of possibility.

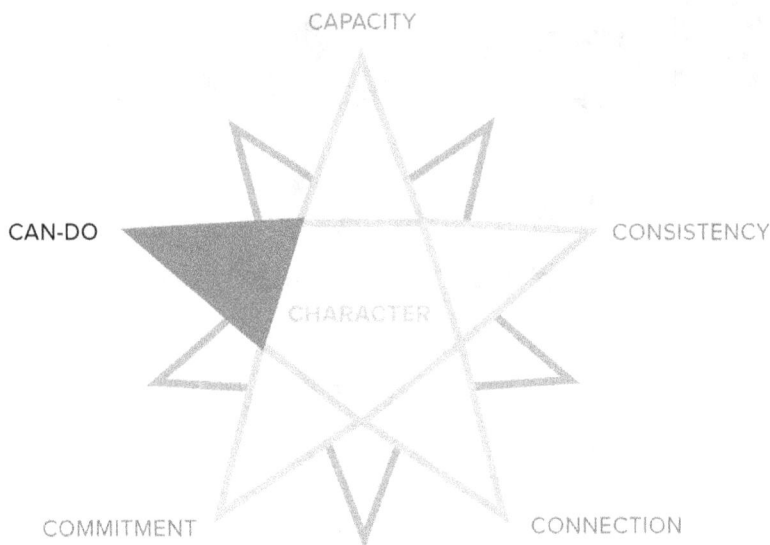

CAPACITY

CAN-DO

CONSISTENCY

CHARACTER

COMMITMENT

CONNECTION

When a new project or opportunity arises, you respond with curiosity and willingness. When a challenge is presented, you calmly shift to resolution mode.

Optimism sets **can-do** people apart. It's why they're so highly valued. They raise the level of energy in a room, inspiring everyone around them to find a way to get things done.

Executives at the top levels of any organization are quick to spot **can-do** people. They're the folks who weigh-in with positive, constructive input when new initiatives come up in meetings. The can't-do people are busy avoiding eye contact, or they speak up primarily to point out flaws in other people's thinking. Can't do people are notable for their apathy and resistance.

Can-do people are:

Open to new things.
Willing to take smart risks.
Unafraid to move forward.

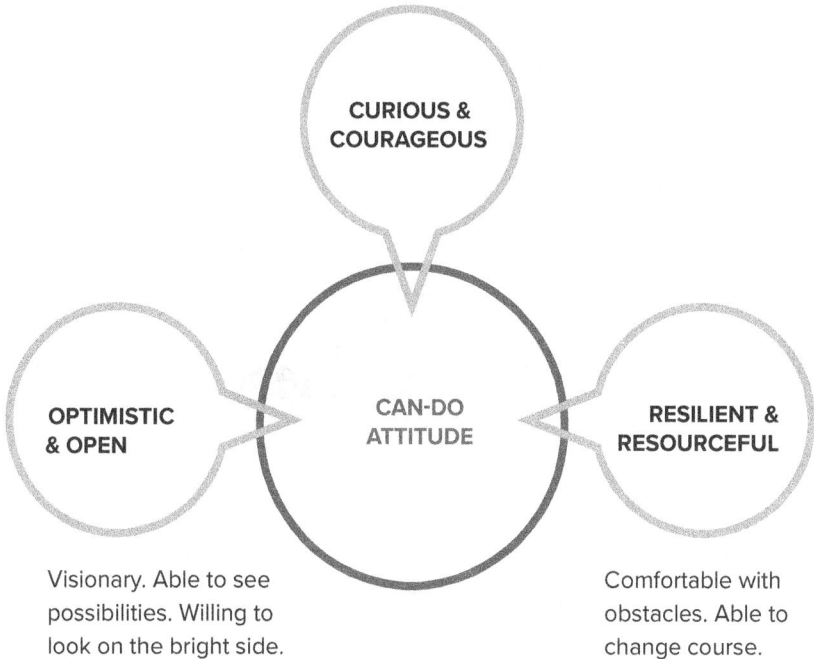

**CURIOUS &
COURAGEOUS**

**OPTIMISTIC
& OPEN**

**CAN-DO
ATTITUDE**

**RESILIENT &
RESOURCEFUL**

Visionary. Able to see
possibilities. Willing to
look on the bright side.

Comfortable with
obstacles. Able to
change course.

Now, let's be clear ... having a **can-do** attitude is not the same as being a
yes-person. If you're a yes-person, you rarely if ever offer a straight-shooting
opinion. You take on random tasks tossed your way because you're afraid
to say no.

A **can-do** person is discerning about their projects and responsibilities,
assuring they are aligned to their personal leadership brand and values.

On a personal level, you can think of a **can-do** attitude as the fuel that
drives you. Without it, your apathy and resistance will prevent you from
shining to your full potential and inspiring others to shine too. Even if you
have capacity, connection, commitment, contribution and character ... if you
don't have a **can-do** attitude, you won't be a true RockStar Leader.

Check Your Optimism Level

There's no bigger drag than a leader who's been beaten down by life, no longer able to muster enthusiasm or optimism. No one wants a leader who's only able to see burdens and challenges.

I beseech you: don't be a negative leader.

It can happen so easily. You get tired of office politics. Your budget gets slashed. Your top two employees quit within weeks of each other. Your kids have the flu and one is failing math.

And what ... you're supposed to sing with joy at the prospect of a brand-spanking new project at work?

Yes. Yes, you are.

Being a RockStar Leader means bringing optimism to the table. It means being wide-open to the possibilities that new ventures may bring.

This responsibility comes with your job title, but I'll grant you it's hard to keep it up all the time.

Has your sense of optimisim waned? Here are 5 key indicators to watch for:

1 When new projects arise, do you find yourself thinking, 'Please no. Why now?!'

2 Do you believe most people in your office are far less practical than you?

3 Are you shocked by the ridiculous ideas people suggest in meetings?

4 When assessing new ideas, do you tend to see far more 'cons' than 'pros?'

5 Are you irritated when someone pops by your office with a 'big new idea?'

If you answered 'yes' to any of these, let it be an alarm bell. You don't want to become a negative leader. You deserve more and so do those around you.

Are You Stuck in a Rut?

There are a million directions you can take your life and career. What stops you from seeing your full spectrum of possibilities?

Having a vibrant sense of possibility changes everything. It puts a bigger perspective on your current situation and a spark of enthusiasm in your heart. Their sense of possibility is why children are brimming with hope and energy.

Adulthood hits and often people let their sense of possibility erode. We're conditioned to think adults should be practical above all else.

So take a good, long look in the mirror. Are you limiting your life for the sake of practicality? How will you feel about that at the end of the road?

Being in a state of possibility makes it easier to move through life. It replaces feelings of dread, burden and complexity that often go hand-in-hand with adulthood.

People with a sense of possibility tend to rise through the ranks of leadership and get the most out of their life because others are drawn to their energy and enthusiasm.

If you are feeling stuck in your career or any aspect of your life, do a gut-check on your possibility level and start opening your mind to a larger reality. The toughest limitations you will ever face in your life exist only as thoughts in your own mind.

Go ahead ... get out of your own way.

Leadership in Tough Times

Let me ask you this: how well do you respond in crisis?

When crisis hits, your abilities as a leader are tested. Big time.

Maybe the economy takes a toll on the business. Or a product fails. Or your biggest customer hits the road.

In moments like these, you have the chance to rise up and be a force of change. You can influence the way others feel and respond. You can be a source of vision and clarity when people desperately need it.

But to do this, you'll probably have to fight some instincts to panic, complain or lay low.

Take an honest look at your natural instincts. Review the statements below and ask yourself how true each one is for you.

When crisis comes calling ...

1 I prefer to keep my head down and wait for trouble to pass.

2 It takes me a long time to get my bearings.

3 I prefer to let someone else take the lead so I won't be blamed for making things worse.

4 I tend to react with anger or fear.

5 I find it hard to be useful.

Now, remembering that leaders are made and not born, ask yourself how you want to be in times of crisis. Come up with 3 - 5 adjectives. Test these adjectives out with a small (or big) issue that arises tomorrow or the next day – take steps to live up to those descriptors.

Notice Your Energy Effect

What happens when you walk in to a room?

Everyone brings their personal energy to meetings, conference calls and interviews – every business encounter.

Some people have the magical effect of raising the energy level in a room. When they're around, people are a little lighter. There's more ease around the table. Problems seem to be resolved quickly and differences of opinion are pleasantly civil.

Other people bring the energy down when they walk into a room. The mood becomes heavier or more serious. Conversations have less flow. There's an air of resistance floating about that causes people to get bogged down. Working together feels like a slog.

It's not your responsibility to set the mood everywhere you go. But you are accountable for what you contribute to energy dynamics.

Are you someone who contributes to flow and ease? Or are you someone who contributes to heaviness and resistance?

To determine your energy effect, ask yourself these 3 questions:

1 Are most of your meetings flowing and light, or heavy and serious?

2 Are most of your phone conversations flowing and light, or heavy and serious?

3 When people end a conversation or meeting with you, do they seem drained?

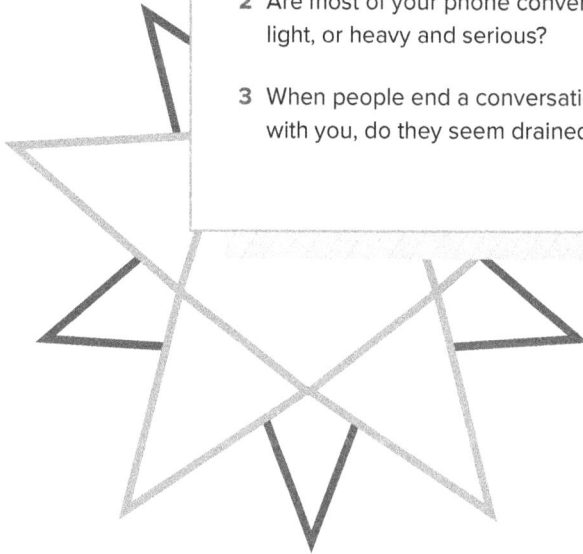

Tune into your trend. If you discover you're bringing a heavy, serious energy wherever you go, make a conscious effort to shift that. Show up to situations with the intention of bringing ease and flow.

Can-Do

LEADING QUESTION

Is my can-do attitude strong enough to make my dreams real?

Character

When you have **character**, you meet whatever life throws at you with clarity and integrity. You have a firm grip on reality.

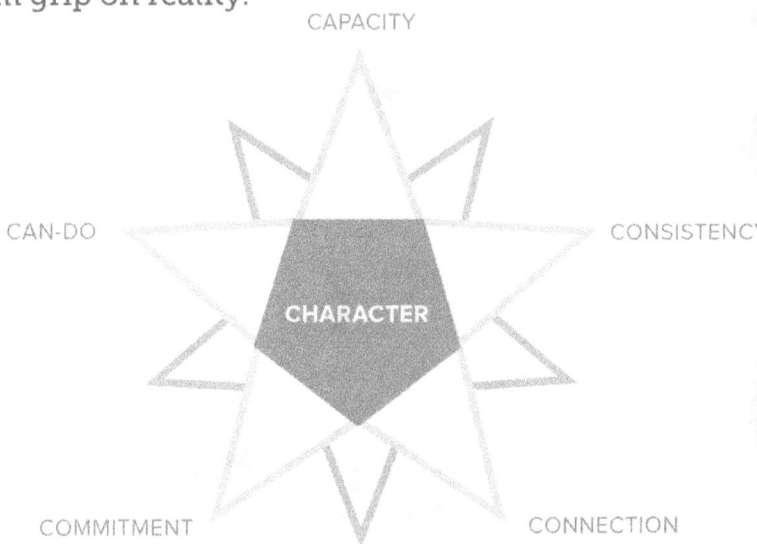

CAPACITY

CAN-DO

CONSISTENC`

CHARACTER

COMMITMENT

CONNECTION

You don't blame others and see yourself as a victim when things go wrong. You look adversity in the eye and say, 'This doesn't define me. I will find a way through this."

Someone with **character** takes the long view and doesn't attach their self-identity to wins or losses. They are stable pillars of objectivity, reason and self-validation no matter what's going on around them.

*For this reason, leaders with **character** shine in any situation. They are compasses that guide others when a challenge or crisis hits.*

When they leave an organization, they are remembered not only for a long list of accomplishments, but also for the friendships they formed and the trust they garnered.

A lack of **character** limits your life. It limits your aptitude as a leader, making it impossible to fulfill your life's purpose or live up to your values.

Lack of **character** can lead you down a dark, unpleasant path that brings out the shadow-side of your personality. Most people have touched into this place at one time or another, to one degree or another. Strengthening your **character** closes the door to your dark side.

While it's not uncommon for people to invest years of training to advance their professional skills or knowledge, it's more unusual for someone to be concertedly devoted to improving their **character.** But the person with deep **character** will ultimately be the better leader.

So I want you to step out from the pack. Take a long, honest look at the state of your **character**, and no matter what you discover, make a commitment to yourself to improve it. It may well be the best gift you ever give yourself.

To be a person of character, you must:

DELIVER RESULTS

Stay focused on achieving results without being swept away by successes or shattered by failures.

EMBRACE ADVERSITY

Manage adversity as elegantly as success. Move through it without feeling victimized or blaming others.

DESIRE GROWTH

Realize that change is a healthy part of life. Flow with it.

SEEK TRUTH

Be unafraid of reality and see it clearly.

BE TRUSTWORTHY

Do what you say you're going to do.
Your word is gold.

There is no limit to how much **character** a RockStar Leader can have. You can continually deepen your integrity and clarity — so I say, go deep.

Question Reality

The tricky thing about denial is you don't know you're in it.

Few people go around thinking, 'Wow, I suspect I'm in denial about important aspects of my life.'

To discover denial, you have to let your mind do a difficult thing. You need to let it question how you see reality.

People with strong character are truth-seekers. They face positive and negative feedback with the same attitude: 'There's definitely something I can learn from this.'

This attitude allows them to see themselves clearly, and evolve more easily than other people.

My client, Dean, embraced the idea of truth seeking with more gusto than I'd ever witnessed. His team had been flailing for months despite his enthusiastic leadership and he was determined to know why.

He asked his team to fill out an anonymous survey, rating his abilities as a leader and sharing their concerns.

He'd sought feedback before, but always in a casual group setting. He was certain his open, carefree personality made it easy for employees to speak candidly. He didn't expect to learn anything earth-shattering from the survey.

He was mistaken.

The results were scathing. It turns out the team had rather a lot to say. His 'enthusiastic' personality was in truth, bombastic.

His 'open,' 'carefree' management style created a chaotic work environment. People were unclear on their job descriptions and goals. The team was rife with interpersonal conflict.

I wondered how Dean would react. True to form, he responded (almost immediately) with his characteristic enthusiasm. I will not lie ... I was pleasantly shocked.

His view was, 'All these people expressing the same concerns can't be wrong.'

Dean has now mended his ways. We've been working together for a while and he's learned to capitalize on his larger than life, throw caution to the wind personality.

He's still the same guy. But now he's learned techniques for being a solid, dependable leader. I'm happy to report his team's performance did a complete turn-around.

Now on to you. Let your mind question reality as you currently see it.

Start by asking these questions:

1 Do you keep having the same arguments with people over and over again?

2 Has someone recently described you in a way that really surprised you?

3 Do people respond to you in a way that's inconsistent with how you see yourself? (i.e., Do they behave as though you're hard-nosed when you think you're easygoing?)

If you answered 'yes,' to any of these questions, your perception of reality could be out of sync.

If you want to take this a step further, try asking 5 people at your workplace to give you 3 words that best describe you, and 3 words that describe your approach to work. If you're shocked by what you hear, it's time to adjust your perceptions. It may also be time to adjust aspects of your behavior.

Test Your Moral Compass

The truth shall set you free, people.

Sure, it's entirely possible to achieve wealth and status by traveling some dark alleys, but you won't have respect or trust. And you may not end your life with satisfaction.

RockStar Leaders are, first and foremost, people of character. People trust them across all levels of the organizations for which they work. Because of this, they can easily rally support for their ideas and deliver big results.

Read the following statements and be real with yourself ... which ones are true for you?

How's your moral compass?

1 I bend the truth to make situations more comfortable for others and myself.

2 I sometimes commit to things I don't plan to fulfill just to get someone off my back.

3 I sometimes take more credit than I deserve.

4 I sometimes make colleagues look bad.

5 I share information 'strategically' to increase the odds of getting what I want.

6 I've been known to bend a lot of rules.

7 I sometimes invent excuses to get a deadline extended.

If any of these statements are true for you, fear not. It's actually shockingly simple to live with more integrity. It's as basic as starting to hold yourself to a higher standard.

You know that slightly icky feeling you get when you're saying or doing something outside of integrity? Listen to that. Stop and change your course. Eventually it becomes your first instinct to act from your highest integrity.

People will start to notice you're someone with strong character. More importantly, so will you.

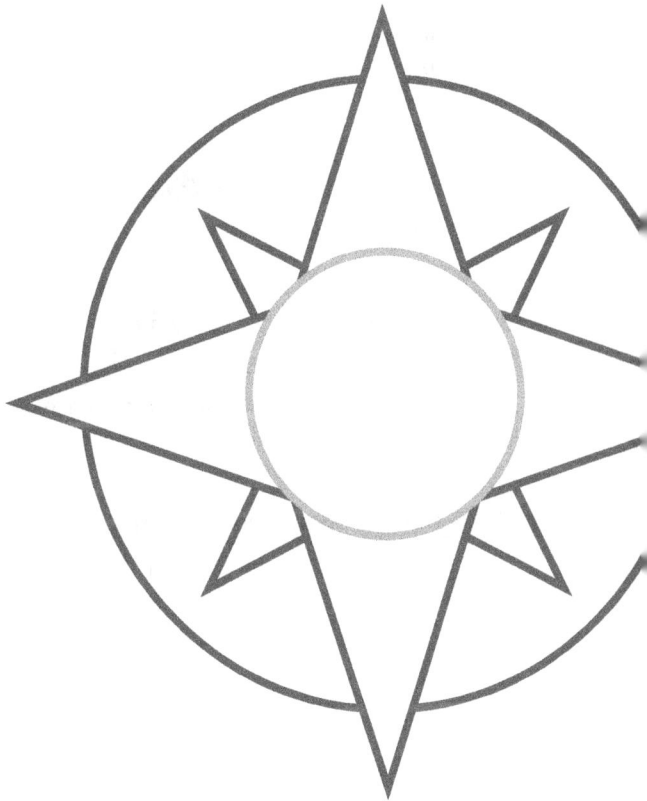

Elegantly Losing

People who are best at life know how to lose.

They move more easily and elegantly through life. They acquire wisdom. They take bigger, smarter risks because they're less afraid of failure.

Good losers take a long-term view, so they're not shattered by disappointments no matter how dramatic they may seem at the time.

I consider elegant losing to be one of the most vital things to teach my teenager who lives in peer culture that values winning above all else.

We have an ongoing conversation about how anyone can be a good winner. But if you don't know how to lose well, you'll get dragged down by life early in the game. You'll start watering down your dreams to spare yourself the pain and discomfort of possible failure.

Successful people know failure is a sage friend. It's a potent source of grit, knowledge, character and humility.

Any wildly accomplished person I've ever met has more than their share of stories about misfires. They achieve greatly because they boldly try things, knowing they can bounce back if they fail.

Less successful people place undue importance on their latest success or failure. They let it define them, and this makes the ground they walk on far less stable.

RockStar Leaders define themselves by the journey, not any fleeting moment of glory or disaster.

Don't Be a Victim

You can't lead with character and vigor if you see yourself as a victim. Simple as that.

When things go wrong in your life, you're responsible. I know that sounds harsh but trust me, when you look at life this way you can take control. Rather than focusing on the external factors that contribute to your problems, you zero in on what you can actually change: you.

When a goal is missed, own it. Figure out what you need to do next time to get a better result and move forward.

Sure, there were likely other people involved in your mishap, but blaming them won't make you a better leader. It will cause you to feel helpless and frustrated. It will make others see you as a victim or complainer.

If you notice that your mind is sometimes consumed by thoughts of what other people have done wrong or how other people need to change, let this be a major warning bell to you.

This expenditure of mental energy will lead you nowhere.

Character

LEADING QUESTION

Do people trust me?

Part Four:

ADVICE FOR
YOUR JOURNEY

3 RockStar Leader Beliefs

Mick Jagger stands apart because he is unabashedly, unapologetically, entirely Mick Jagger. I think the same could be said for Adele or Neil Young, Kanye West or Stevie Nicks.

There isn't one particular way to be a rock star. It's about knowing who you are and having the courage to say, 'I gotta be me.'

The same can be said for being a RockStar Leader. It's easy to read about it. It's lovely to contemplate it. But you need to be tough as nails to journey inward and be completely honest about what you see.

And it takes guts and determination to live the RockStar Leader Skills every single day.

I want to talk to you about the difference between just 'doing' the skills and 'being' a RockStar Leader.

*'Doing' the skills – understanding and practicing them – is a tremendous starting point. It will bring you some degree of success and growth. But to be a true RockStar Leader, you need to believe in your heart (not just your mind) that the 6 skills are a **way of being** that you choose.*

Do you choose to show up in the world as someone who lives these skills?

Over my career as a leadership coach, I've seen people who struggled to embrace these skills as a way of being. They agreed with them intellectually, but they often made decisions that were at odds with them. They saw them as intriguing concepts rather than a way of life.

People like Sam ('A RockStar Story,' page 8), who went from career uncertainty to career fulfillment in 6 months, do more than just change their behaviors.

They change their mindsets. They take charge of their careers using the 6 RockStar Leader Skills.

RockStar Leaders live by these beliefs:

1 I take responsibility for my leadership and life.

2 I strive to be the best I can be.

3 I will shine brightly and help others shine too.

BELIEF 1: I take responsibility for my leadership and life.

Don't take these words lightly: You're in charge of your life. You're the only one that can steer the direction of your career.

As a leader, you're continually faced with competing priorities. It's the nature of blending leading and living. You need to make some tradeoffs.

It's up to you to choose what's best for you at work and at home. Don't shy away from that responsibility.

For example, if your career is disappointing you, choose to fix it. Letting go of blame will change every aspect of your life. So let go.

When I need to remind myself of this, I recall the image of my son's first grade concert. Picture 50 six-year-olds loudly singing the words, 'If it is to be, it's up to me.' We didn't all get this information at age 6. But it's never to late to take charge.

BELIEF 2: I strive to be the best I can be.

You're skilled and talented. Own it.

You possess your own unique, distinct brand of greatness. It combines talents and attributes you were born with and some you acquired.

The point is, you're the only person in the universe who's lived your life and possesses all of your qualities combined.

Don't underplay, resist or deny your excellence. Honor it. Use it. And most importantly, continually improve upon it.

Always look for opportunities to enhance your existing skills and acquire new ones. Don't settle for status quo.

Let me be totally blunt, you can't be a RockStar Leader without a burning desire for self-growth.

BELIEF 3: I will shine brightly and help others shine too.

Let your awesomeness soar. Make your value visible so you can write your own ticket in life.

Let's be clear: this is not about shameless self promotion or anything remotely like it. It's about standing out among the crowd in a positive way so you can fully offer your unique talents to the world.

Don't hold back to make others comfortable. Instead, use your leadership skills to help them shine too.

It's entirely possible (and advisable) to shine brightly with humility. There's a clear line between confidence and arrogance. Walk it.

Rock On

Congratulations. You've gained insight into what it takes to be a RockStar Leader.

Regardless of your current skill level or job title, you can raise the caliber of your leadership through these skills.

As you reach the end of this book, remember this is really the beginning of your next performance. Now go forth. It's my hope that you will take these skills into your daily life, perpetually expanding your ability to deliver, lead and inspire. I also hope you truly make them your own, living them in a way that fits with your unique personality.

The RockStar Leader Skills are your road to the new career security. They can blow the door wide open for your career options by allowing people to see who you really are and what you have to offer.

To use these skills to your full advantage, keep fine-tuning each one in equal measure. Remember they work as an integrated system.

RockStar Leaders are the most sought-after people in the business world. So go for it. Don't hold back.

Make your performance shine.

Lisa

P.S. I love feedback. Please share your thoughts directly with me at:
lisa@lisamartininternational.com

Afterword

May I make a suggestion?

If you found this book of value, consider bringing the leadership development program, *LEAD: 6 Skills to Be a RockStar Leader,* to your organization.

Just like this book, **LEAD** offers pragmatic skills to help individuals rise to the challenges and opportunities they face in the workplace.

Program participants become more self-aware and learn how to continually make their performance and their organization's performance shine. It's ideal for all levels of employees.

LEAD is a flexible, turnkey licensing solution that comes with all the tools required to cultivate high-impact, thriving leaders.

In other words, you get a proven program with all the training materials you need, including online 360 assessments, facilitator guides, workbooks, PowerPoint Decks, posters and, of course, this book.

And you have the freedom to deliver **LEAD** your way on your schedule.

Acknowledgments

To the rock stars who taught me what it means to be a RockStar Leader.

In the mid-90s, I sold my upstart PR firm to one of Canada's largest agencies as they expanded across the country.

I signed on as their youngest partner. My mandate was clear: help the company become the biggest player in the market by building a kick-ass Vancouver team. I knew we'd need to attract the best people in the city to achieve this goal.

I went about the business of recruiting, hiring and mentoring rock star talent. I instinctively knew the type of people I needed: people who cared about delivering value. People with a burning sense they could achieve whatever they set their minds to.

My single-mindedness paid off. We quickly built a team that rivaled even our most established competitors. After 9 months of operation, we were cited as the third most profitable PR agency in the city. We never looked back.

Those rock stars proved my theory that anything is possible with the right people on your team. They were tried and true RockStar Leaders. I appreciate you all...and the many rock star colleagues I've worked with since then.

Of course, a big thanks to my clients. Thanks for letting me be a part of your leadership journey. You've taught me so much.

This rather incomplete list of authors have influenced, informed and inspired my thinking generally, but also specifically on the concept of being a RockStar Leader: Marcus Buckingham, Michael Bungay Stainer, Dr. Henry Cloud, Nancy Duarte, Seth Godin, Marshall Goldsmith, Daniel Goleman, Sheryl Sandberg, Susan Scott, Tom Rath, and Benjamin Zander & Rosamund Stone Zander. I've devoured their words.

And lastly, a heartfelt thank you to all you rock star readers for spending your precious gift of time to absorb these words. You rock!

About the Author
Lisa Martin, PCC

Lisa Martin has made it her mission to help companies keep and cultivate leaders. She's the creator of the *Lead + Live Better*™ leadership programs; author of 5 books, including the bestselling *Briefcase Moms*; and a seasoned speaker, facilitator and executive coach.

For the past 15 years Lisa has designed and delivered leadership programs for PwC, TELUS, Vancouver Canucks, HSBC and UBC, to name a few.

Her powerful, easy-to-use *Lead + Live Better*™ turnkey leadership licensing solutions empower organizations to cultivate amazing leaders at every level.

She has coached thousands of people on the art of thriving as a leader and in life, and counseled companies on building leadership capacity.

As a speaker, Lisa is sought by international conferences, corporations and universities. She's known for her fun, straight-shooting speaking style and her intuitive sense for her audience.

She does all this as the founder of *Lisa Martin International*, a boutique leadership development firm with global scope, which equips organizations to deliver powerful leadership development in-house.

Lisa lives in North Vancouver with her husband, spirited teenaged son and two cats that act like toddlers.

You can find her at: **lisamartininternational.com**

"The brighter you shine, the more options you have in life. Think of it as star power."

Lisa Martin

Cornerview Press
Box 30075
North Vancouver, BC
Canada V7H 2Y8

Editor Jacqueline Voci
Cover and text design by Melissa Hicks & Melanie Iu
Cover image by Getty Images
Author Photo by Linda Mackie

ISBN 978-0-9734560-1-1

Library of Congress information is available on request.

The examples I've used in this book reflect the stories I've been privileged to share in my work as a leadership coach. To respect my clients' privacy, I have changed their names and other identifying details.

lisa MARTIN

LEAD+LIVE BETTER

Lisa's Lead+Live Better™ programs deliver advanced leadership and life skills in a fun, intuitive and straight-shooting way.

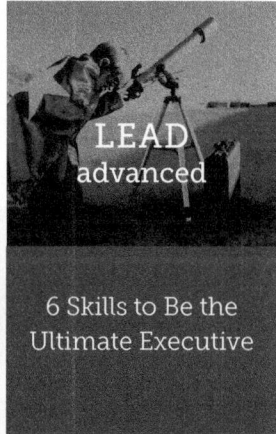

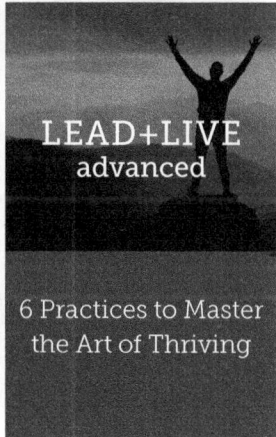

LEAD

6 Skills to Be a RockStar Leader

LEAD advanced

6 Skills to Be the Ultimate Executive

LEAD for women

Briefcase Moms

LEAD+LIVE

6 Practices to Live Bigger

LEAD+LIVE advanced

6 Practices to Master the Art of Thriving

lisamartininternational.com

www.ingramcontent.com/pod-product-compliance
Lightning Source LLC
Chambersburg PA
CBHW060323220326
41598CB00027B/4403